A nursery history of England

Elizabeth O'Neill

LITTLE MEN AND BIG BEASTS.—The very first men who lived in England and Scotland were very little. They were most likely quite wild and savage and they had to fight against many big animals—bigger than any we know to-day. These ran about everywhere.

A NURSERY HISTORY of ENGLAND.

By ELIZABETH O'NEILL.

Pictures by George Morrow.

NEW YORK

FREDERICK A. STOKES COMPANY

PUBLISHERS

TO

MARY, BETTY & BILL

THE BRITONS AND THEIR POETS

A LONG time after the days of the little men and big beasts there were some people called the Britons, who were not quite wild and savage, but they did everything in quite different ways from those in which we do them now. There were many kings among the Britons, and the people fought for their kings against other people and their kings. They spent a great deal of time in fighting. They were very big and strong, and had golden hair and blue eyes. They did not wear many clothes, and the men stained themselves blue. They had men of whom they thought a great deal called "Bards," who made and sang poetry for them. On

A BRITON

the night before a fight the bards would sing to the soldiers songs about other brave soldiers in earlier times, and this made the men want to fight bravely in the battle. The Britons had not any big towns, and their houses were very small, the walls made of mud. When they were not fighting the Britons hunted animals a great deal, and afterwards they ate them. They also grew corn and things to make bread.

THE BRITISH PRIESTS

A DRUID SACRIFICE

The Britons did not know rightly about God. They thought there were a great many gods, and they used to say prayers to them among oak-trees. They even said prayers to things which were not alive, such as fire and water, and they thought a great deal of the mistletoe, which often grew on the oak-trees. They had priests called "Druids," who were the cleverest of all the Britons. They used to wear long white dresses

On special feast days they used to cut pieces of mistletoe with long golden knives, and give them out to the people, who thought that they kept them from being sick or unhappy. On the same day the Druids used to kill and burn great white oxen to please their gods.

7

A BRITISH WAR CHARIOT

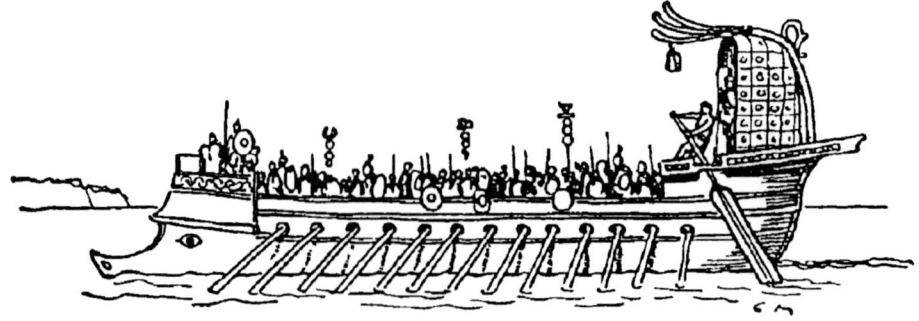

A ROMAN WAR GALLEY

JULIUS CÆSAR AND THE BRITONS

A ROMAN SOLDIER

The great Roman soldier, Julius Cæsar, came to Britain. When he lived the people who lived in Rome were fighting against many other countries, and generally won the battles. Julius Cæsar had heard about the Britons, who had helped the people in France to fight against him, and he made up his mind to come and see the country, and if he could, win it for the Roman people. He came across the sea with soldiers in big ships called galleys, and the Britons went down to the seashore to try to keep them away. They had helmets on their heads, and big shields made of basketwork covered with animals' skins. They threw stones and sharp things at the Romans when they tried to get on shore. At first the Romans were afraid, but one of them, who carried a pole with an eagle on it (which the Romans had as we have our flag), jumped into the water and waded to the shore. They fought bravely, and so did the Britons, but the Romans won. Cæsar went away again, but came back next year.

CARACTACUS, A BRAVE BRITON

Julius Cæsar came a second time to Britain, but he did not really get it for Rome. Nearly a hundred years afterwards the Emperor Claudius sent soldiers from Rome to fight against the Britons. One of the bravest of the British kings, named Caractacus, fought for many years against the Romans, but at last his stepmother gave him up to them. They took him in chains to Rome. When he saw the big houses and beautiful streets of Rome, which was the greatest city in the world, he wondered why the Romans had come to take his own poor country from him. When he was taken to see the Emperor Claudius, Caractacus told the Emperor what he was thinking. The Emperor thought him such a brave and great man that he told the soldiers to let him go free. So Caractacus was set free, but we do not know whether he ever came back to his own country again.

A ROMAN STANDARD-BEARER

10

AN EARLY ENGLISH GALLEY

BOADICEA, THE BRITISH QUEEN

It took the Romans many years to win Britain quite for themselves, for the British kings, and sometimes the queens, fought so bravely. The bravest queen of all was Boadicea, a beautiful woman, with golden hair and blue eyes. The Romans had actually whipped her, and been very rough with her two daughters. Boadicea was terribly angry, and she went about telling the other Britons and begging them to fight their hardest against the Romans. She herself fought in a great battle, riding in a little chariot, or carriage, with small horses, which the Britons used when they were fighting. But in the middle of the fight she saw that the Romans were winning. Rather than be taken prisoner by them she killed herself by drinking poison.

STANDARD OF THE WHITE HORSE

THE FIRST ENGLISHMEN IN BRITAIN

In the end the Romans got Britain for themselves, and some of them came to live here. There were Romans in Britain for nearly 400 years, but by that time the people of Rome were having a great deal of trouble, and had to fight many battles. They wanted their soldiers from Britain and took them away, and so the Britons were free once more. But they no longer knew how to fight well, and when some people called Picts and Scots from Scotland came to fight against the Britons, they had to ask help from other people. The British King, Vortigern, asked two kings who used to fight on the sea to come to help him. They were called Englishmen, and they were the first Englishmen to settle down and live in Britain. They were named Hengist and Horsa. When they had helped the Britons they would not go away again, and many more Englishmen came from the country across the sea where they lived, and after a time they won the country from the Britons, and so Britain became England.

AN ENGLISH SOLDIER

14

THE GREAT KING ARTHUR

The Englishmen had to fight for many years before they won all Britain for themselves. At last most of the Britons were chased into the country we now call Wales. One of the bravest British kings who fought against the Englishmen was the great King Arthur. He was one of the best kings who have ever been. He tried to choose only brave and good men to fight for him. They were called King Arthur's Knights, and they were kind and gentle as well as brave, and they were especially good to women and children. They fought against bad men. King Arthur used sometimes to send his knights to do brave things far away from home, but he liked best to have them in his palace. In the big room where the king used to eat there was a very big round table, and the king was happiest when he had all his knights sitting round it. They would tell tales of the wonderful things they had seen and done.

AN EARLY ENGLISH KING

ST. GREGORY AND THE ENGLISH CHILDREN

AN EARLY ENGLISH
GENTLEMAN

At first the Englishmen were not all under one king. There were many kings, and they and their people fought against each other. Often the men who were taken prisoners, and even the women and children, were made to work as slaves. Sometimes they were sold to men who came over the seas to buy them. One day some little English slave children were standing ready to be sold in the market-place at Rome when a good priest named Gregory passed by and saw them. They were so pretty, with their blue eyes and pink-and-white faces, that he asked who they were. Some one told him that they were "Angli," which was the Roman way of saying "English." He said they were more like "Angeli," which was the Roman way of saying "Angels."

When he heard that the English people did not know about God, he made up his mind to come and tell them about Him; but he was soon made Pope, or head of the Church, and he had to stay in Rome. But Pope Gregory the Great never forgot the English children, and he soon sent some one to tell the English people about God.

B

EARLY ENGLISH PEOPLE AT TABLE

ST. AUGUSTINE AND THE ENGLISH

The English people used to say prayers to many gods just as the Britons did, but their gods were different. They thought that thunder was a god, and they prayed to Woden, the god of war. But Pope Gregory sent a very good man, who was one of his friends, to tell them about God. This man was named Augustine, and we now call him St. Augustine. He came over the sea from Rome with other holy men, and went first to a king named Æthelbert, whose wife, Bertha, already knew about God. She had come from France to marry Æthelbert, and all his people were baptized and became Christians, which meant that they now knew about God, and said the prayers and did the good things which St. Augustine told them to do. After a time all the other kings and all the English people became Christians too.

ST. AUGUSTINE

AN EARLY ENGLISH WOMAN

EDWIN, A GREAT ENGLISH KING

One of the greatest English kings in those early days was Edwin, who lived in the north of England near Scotland. He had part of Scotland, too, in his kingdom, and he built Edinburgh, which was called after him. He kept all his people in good order, and everything and everybody was safe. He used to travel about from one part of his kingdom to another, to see for himself that things were in good order. He used to be dressed very beautifully, and took many servants with him. A purple banner, ornamented with gold, used to be carried before him, and a long spear with a bunch of feathers fastened to it. Edwin wanted to show the people how great the king was, so that they would obey him, and be happy and peaceful.

23

A SOLDIER IN KING ALFRED'S TIME

AN OLD ENGLISH WAGGON

A COWHERD WHO WAS A POET

After all the English had become Christians, many men who wanted to be especially good used to join together and live in big houses called monasteries. They were called monks, and they spent their time in working and saying prayers, and they all did exactly what the head monk told them to do. Sometimes women lived in the same way in houses called convents. The women were called nuns. Sometimes, but not often, a woman was head of a monastery. At a monastery in a town called Whitby there was a very good nun called Hilda, who was head over a convent and a monastery. At the monastery there was a poor servant who used to look after the cows. He had never been to school, and did not know very much. He was very quiet and shy. Sometimes the servants would have feasts together, and each one would be asked to play on the harp and sing. Once at a feast when Cædmon saw the harp coming to him, he was so frightened that he got up and ran away. He threw himself on his straw bed very miserable and ashamed. Yet he was a real poet, and that very night he began to make

AN OLD ENGLISH MINSTREL · a beautiful poem about God, and the making of the world. When Hilda heard what wonderful poetry he made, she told him he should become a monk. He did, and was a very holy and good one, and he wrote a great deal of beautiful poetry, which was written down and read by all the Englishmen who could read.

THE FIRST ENGLISHMAN WHO WROTE HISTORY

Another great monk about this time was Bede, who lived in a monastery at a town called Jarrow. He was not a poet like Cædmon, but wrote a history of the English people, and turned some Latin writings into English, so that the people could understand them. When he was ill and going to die he was anxious to finish a piece of work which he had begun. This was to put part of the great book called the Bible into English. He could not write, as he was too ill, but he lay in bed and told a young monk what words to write. At last the young monk said, "Master, it is now finished." Bede answered, "*All* is now finished," and in a very few minutes he died.

AN ENGLISH MONK SAYING HIS PRAYERS

26

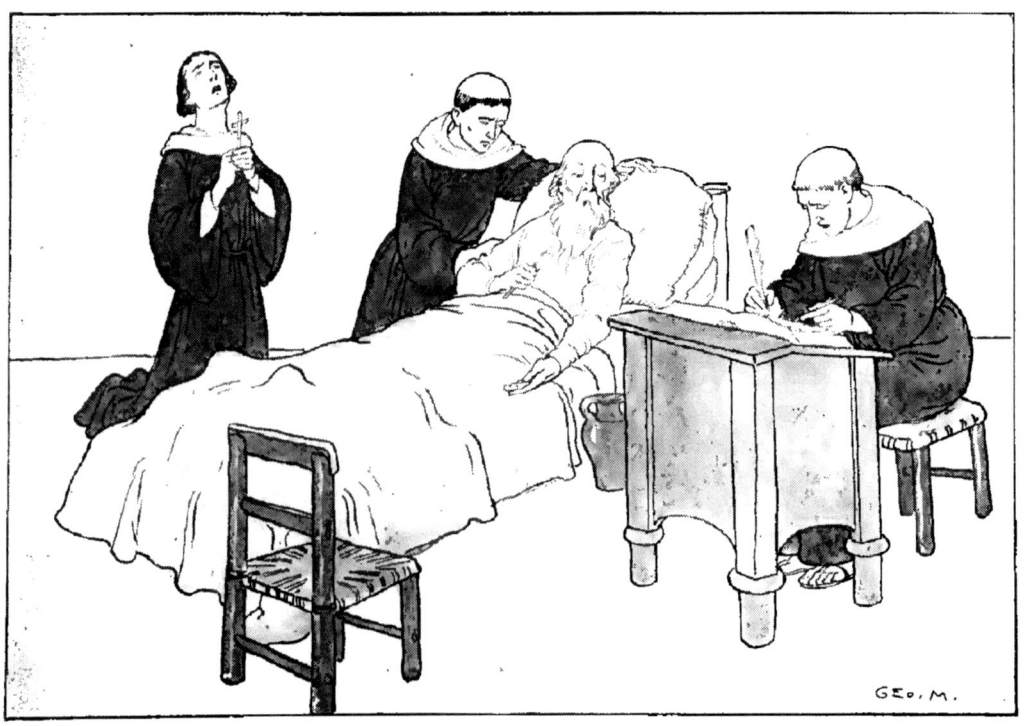

A HARPER

A KING WHO WAS A CLEVER BOY

Most of the clever men in early England were monks. But there was one very clever man who was not a monk, but a king This was the great King Alfred. In those days very few children learned to read. Even the sons of kings could not read or write. They spent most of their time in learning to hunt and fight. But Alfred's mother, Queen Osburga, wanted her sons to be clever men as well as brave. Alfred had three older brothers. One day the queen called her boys to her and showed them a beautiful book. She promised to give it to the one who should first be able to read it. They all began to learn to read from the clever men in their father's court; but Alfred, though he was the youngest, worked hardest. He was soon able to read, and his mother gave him the beautiful book.

A DANISH SOLDIER

KING ALFRED AND THE DANES

When Alfred grew up he became king. England in those days was troubled by some fierce men, who came over the sea in ships. They were called "Danes." They would come on land and steal all the best things from the houses and churches, and carry them off in their ships. Often they set fire to places, and burnt up the corn in the fields. After a time they came in great numbers and tried to take the land away from the English, just as the English had taken it from the Britons. At first Alfred had to run away and hide from the Danes; but he was determined to fight them, and make them do his will. He dressed himself up as a man who played the harp, and went right in among the Danish soldiers, to find out what they were going to do.

A DANISH SHIP

30

KING ALFRED AND THE CAKES

At one time when King Alfred was hiding from the Danes he stayed with a poor man and his wife in a little cottage. The woman did not know that he was the King. She thought he was a very lazy young man to sit all day doing nothing. Alfred was really thinking how he could fight the Danes. One day the woman asked Alfred to watch some cakes which she was cooking, and to see that they did not burn while she went away to do some other work. Alfred was thinking so much about other things that he forgot all about the cakes, and they were burnt black. The woman was so angry that she gave Alfred a good hard slap. Alfred only laughed at the idea of a king being whipped.

AN EARLY ENGLISH FARMER

AN EARLY ENGLISH WOOD-CUTTER

THE BAPTISM OF THE DANISH KING

At last Alfred got together a great many brave soldiers, and he took them to fight against the Danes. He won many battles, and at last the fighting stopped. Alfred gave the Danes a big part of England for themselves, and they promised not to steal or burn any more They were not Christians before, but they became Christians now Guthrum, their King, was baptized, and Alfred was his godfather, and for many years the English and the Danes lived happily side by side, and the people were peaceful and glad.

35   c

AN EARLY ENGLISH HORSEMAN

KING EDGAR THE PEACEFUL

There were many great kings after Alfred,
and they even got power again over that part
of England which had been given to the Danes.
One of these kings was named Edgar. He was
called Edgar the Peaceful; but he made all the
other kings in England say that he was the chief
king. The King of Scotland had to say so too,
and one day he and five other kings showed how
much they thought of Edgar when they rowed
him with their own hands down the river Dee
to the Church of St. John at Chester.

AN EARLY ENGLISH KING

THE GOOD KING CNUT

After many years more fierce Danes began
to come across the sea to rob and burn. Un-
fortunately, the king in those days was not
brave and active like Alfred. He was called
Ethelred the Unready. In the end Danish
kings got England for themselves, though not
many Danes came with them. The English
people were not chased away, but they had
Danes and not Englishmen for kings One of
these kings, a great and good man, was named
Cnut Sometimes people say things to kings
and princes which are not true, just to please
them; but Cnut did not like people to do this
with him. One day he was sitting on the seashore when the sea was rolling in over the
sands. Some of Cnut's servants said to him
that the waves would not wet so great a king.
Cnut knew that this was nonsense, and he sat
until the waves rolled over his feet and wet his
clothes. Then he turned to the foolish people
and scolded them gently for their flattery.

KING CNUT

39

AN EARLY ENGLISHMAN
SHOOTING BIRDS

KING HAROLD

EARL HAROLD AND DUKE WILLIAM

After a short time England had English kings again. The last of these was named Harold. He was a very brave and beautiful man. Once, before he was king, he was in a ship which was wrecked on the shores of a country called Normandy. The chief man of this country was called Duke William. Harold was saved from the wreck; but Duke William kept him in prison until he would promise to help him to become King of England, when Edward, the English king, should die. Harold swore an oath, which is a sort of promise which it is a dreadful thing to break. While he promised he had to put his hand on a kind of altar under which were the bones of saints. Harold did not know until after he had promised that these bones were there. William told him afterwards, thinking that he would be too frightened to break his oath. Then Harold went back to England.

AN EARLY ENGLISH SOLDIER

THE BATTLE OF HASTINGS

Soon after Harold had sworn his oath the English king died, and the Englishmen chose Harold to be their king. When Duke William was told that Harold had broken his oath, he was very angry, and he brought a great army of soldiers over to England to fight Harold. Harold had just finished another battle in a part of the country far away from Hastings, the place where Duke William came. He led his army down to Hastings, and setting up his flag, he gathered his soldiers round it, and a great battle was fought. It lasted all day. Harold and his men fought bravely, though they were tired out with their long march. At last Duke William told some of his soldiers to shoot upwards with their sharp arrows, so that they would stick into the heads of the Englishmen. King Harold was hurt in the eye with an arrow, and fell back dead. So William won the battle, and became King of England.

WILLIAM THE CONQUEROR

42

A NORMAN CASTLE

HEREWARD THE WAKE

ENGLISH DEER

After William was crowned King of England there were still many Englishmen who said they would not have him for their king. William, who was called William the Conqueror, because he won all the battles he fought, fought many of these Englishmen and killed them. He was so angry with them that he burnt down all the houses in one large part of England, and killed all the people, so that for a long time that part of the land was left quite quiet, and nobody lived there. The bravest of the Englishmen, however, went to the island of Ely, a small piece of land with very soft watery land all round it. It was very hard for William to get to them; but at last he built a kind of stone bridge across the soft land, and so reached the "Camp of Refuge." That is what the strong place which the Englishmen had built was called. William had a great many soldiers, and the brave Englishmen had to give themselves up. The chief of them was Hereward, who was called Hereward "the Wake," or "Watchful."

THE DEATH OF THE RED KING

The next King of England after William the Conqueror was his son William. He was a very strong and nice-looking man, like his father, but he had a red face, and rather reddish hair, and so he was called "Rufus," or the "Red King" He was not such a good man as his father, and was cruel to his people. He was very fond of hunting animals, like his father was. William the Conqueror had taken a great forest, and made it his own. He had even pulled down houses in it, so that he could chase the deer without anyone coming in his way One day when the Red King was hunting in the "New Forest" his arrow just missed a big deer. William was very excited, and called out to his friend, Walter Tyrel, to shoot the deer Walter let an arrow fly, but by accident it stuck in the king's eye, and he fell dead. Walter was so frightened that he rode away, and the king's body lay all day in the forest, until in the evening it was carried away in a workman's cart, and buried in the big church at a town called Winchester. Some people said that this sudden death was a punishment to the Red King for his cruelty, and for the way in which his father had made the forest.

A WOOD-CUTTER IN THE NEW FOREST

RALPH FLAMBARD'S ESCAPE FROM THE TOWER

When the Red King died, his brother Henry was crowned king. He was the first King of England who had that name, and so he was called Henry I. He was a good king, and kind to his people; but he punished bad men. The man who had most helped the Red King to be cruel was a bishop named Ralph Flambard. King Henry shut him up in the great Tower of London, which was used as a prison for such people. The king wanted to keep him from doing any more cruel things to the people. Ralph was very cunning, and he got some people to send him a very long and strong rope. This was put inside a barrel of beer which was sent to Ralph. He tied it to a bar of his window, and slid down it, and so got safely away. After a while King Henry forgave him; but he was never able to do any more harm to the people.

A NORMAN LADY

DUKE ROBERT OF NORMANDY

King Henry I had a brother Robert, who was older than himself. He had not been made king because he was rather a lazy man, but he was Duke of Normandy, the country from which William the Conqueror had come. Duke Robert was a very brave soldier, and a very beautiful man; but he never knew exactly what he wanted to do. He suddenly thought he would like to be King of England; but King Henry took English soldiers over the sea to Normandy, and they fought against Robert's Norman soldiers, at a place called Tenchebrai. The English won the battle, and the English soldiers were pleased to have conquered the Normans, for they hated to remember how Norman soldiers had conquered the English at Hastings. Poor Duke Robert was taken prisoner, and kept in prison in England for many years until he died.

A NORMAN SOLDIER

51

D

OLD ENGLISH PEASANTS

THE WRECK OF THE *WHITE SHIP*

Henry I had one only son, William, and he loved him very much. One day, when the king and his son were coming back to England from France, they were just going on their ship when the captain of another ship, called the *White Ship*, begged them to go with him. The king said he would not; but William, to please the captain, went on the *White Ship* with one of his sisters and many friends. William gave the sailors a great deal of beer to drink. This was a mistake, for they became so excited that they did not know what they were doing, and although the sea was beautifully still, and it was a moonlight night, the sailors let the ship go against a rock, and it was wrecked. William was put in a boat, and was rowed away from the ship; but when he found that his sister was not with him he made the sailors row back, and so many people jumped on the boat that it went down into the water. So did the *White Ship*, and everybody was drowned except one poor butcher. King Henry was so sad when he heard of his son's death that he never again was seen to smile.

A NORMAN SOLDIER

QUEEN MATILDA'S ESCAPE FROM OXFORD

When King Henry no longer had a son he was very anxious that his daughter Matilda should be made queen when he died. A great many Englishmen promised to have her as queen; but when Henry died they broke their promise, and made her cousin, Stephen, king. Matilda fought against Stephen for many years. One time she was shut up in a town called Oxford. There was very little to eat, and the queen wanted to get away without Stephen's soldiers catching her. It was winter, and the ground was covered with snow, so Matilda and the soldiers who went with her wrapped themselves in white cloaks, so that Stephen's soldiers should not see them as they would have done if they had worn dark clothes. In the end Stephen was king till he died, and Matilda's son, Henry, then became king. He was called Henry II.

QUEEN MATILDA

55

GEOFFREY PLANTAGENET, THE
FATHER OF KING HENRY II

TENTS OF NORMAN SOLDIERS

THE DEATH OF ST. THOMAS BECKET

A NORMAN KNIGHT

King Henry II was a good king too; but he was very easily made angry, and then he did and said things which he was very sorry for after. He had a great friend called Thomas Becket. Thomas was a priest, and King Henry made him head over all the churches and priests in England. He lived at Canterbury, where there was a big church called a cathedral. He was then called Archbishop of Canterbury. King Henry quarrelled with Thomas, because the king wanted him to do things which he did not think would be good for the church. One day, when the king was in France, he said some very angry things about the archbishop, and some of his knights and soldiers, when they heard him, came over to England, and killed the archbishop in his own church at Canterbury. He was very good and very brave, and when he was dead he was called St. Thomas of Canterbury.

KING HENRY'S PENANCE

The soldiers who killed Becket thought that King Henry had wanted them to do so, and would be glad. But Henry was very sad indeed, and very vexed with himself for having said angry things about the archbishop Thomas was buried in his own cathedral at Canterbury, and an altar was put over his grave. King Henry went to the grave, and to show how sorry he was, he got the monks to whip him while he was there, and when they had finished he knelt all night saying his prayers before the altar. He never forgot that it was through his angry words that St. Thomas had been killed.

A BISHOP

58

BERENGARIA, QUEEN OF
RICHARD I

A KNIGHT'S PRAYERS

A CRADLE IN THE TIME OF KING HENRY II

The soldiers who killed St. Thomas were cruel and bad-tempered, but they ought to have known better. For in those days the knights or chief soldiers were taught to be good and gentle, as well as brave. The day when a young soldier was made a knight was a very important one in his life. Generally he stayed in church all during the night before, with his sword and shield in front of him. He spent the night saying prayers that he would be able to be good, and fight only wicked people, and help women and children as a good knight should.

THE WINNING OF IRELAND

It was in the time of King Henry II that Englishmen first tried to get Ireland to let the English king rule over them. Ireland is very near England, with a little sea between, and the English thought it would be a good thing if they could join together as one country. The Irish people were very lively, and very kind when they liked people; but long after England had only one king, the Irish people had a great many, and the kings and the people fought each other a great deal. They quarrelled so much that Englishmen thought they would settle things for them, and Henry II went over to Ireland and got many of the Irish kings to say they would have him as king over them. He sat in a wooden palace, near Dublin, the chief place in Ireland, and the Irish chiefs and kings came and knelt before him because he was their king.

AN IRISH CHIEFTAIN

KING RICHARD OF THE LION HEART

When Henry II died his son Richard became King of England. He was such a brave soldier that he was called "Richard of the Lion Heart" He did not stay long in England, but went with other great kings and princes and many soldiers to a far-off land called Palestine, where Our Lord's tomb or grave was. The Holy Tomb had been taken away from the Christians by some fierce dark men called the Turks. They did not understand about Our Lord, and they would not let people go to say their prayers at the Tomb. But Richard and the others went to fight them, and this was called a crusade. The soldiers wore a red cross on their shields to remind them of Our Lord. Richard was very ill when he got to Palestine; but he made his men carry him right in among the fighting so that he could tell them what to do. In the end the Turks were forced to let people go to say their prayers at the Tomb.

A KNIGHT GOING ON A CRUSADE

ROBIN HOOD AND THE SHERIFF OF NOTTINGHAM

While King Richard was far away his brother John was the chief man in England. But he was a foolish and bad man, and people were not happy. Some people even ran away and hid in the woods for fear he would do them harm. One of these was a young gentleman named Robin Hood. John had taken his house and all his things away from him, and Robin was very angry.

AN ARCHER

He made up his mind to hide in the woods, and he got other men to go with him, and they were all very happy and merry. They used to take money from rich people and give it to the poor, and though they were rough with proud people they would never hurt women or, of course, children. Robin was so kind and merry that we cannot help liking him. He was always doing funny things. There was one man who hated him very much. This was the chief man in a place called Nottingham. He was called the Sheriff. One day Robin dressed himself up as a butcher and sold meat at the market in Nottingham. The Sheriff said he would go back to his home with him and buy some of his cows: but Robin took him into the Forest, and called all his merry men to him. They gave the Sheriff a very good dinner, but they took all the money he had with him. There were three hundred pounds, which means thousands of pennies. Then they let the Sheriff go home. He was dreadfully sad about his money, and angry with himself for believing that Robin was only a butcher.

AN OLD ENGLISH GAME

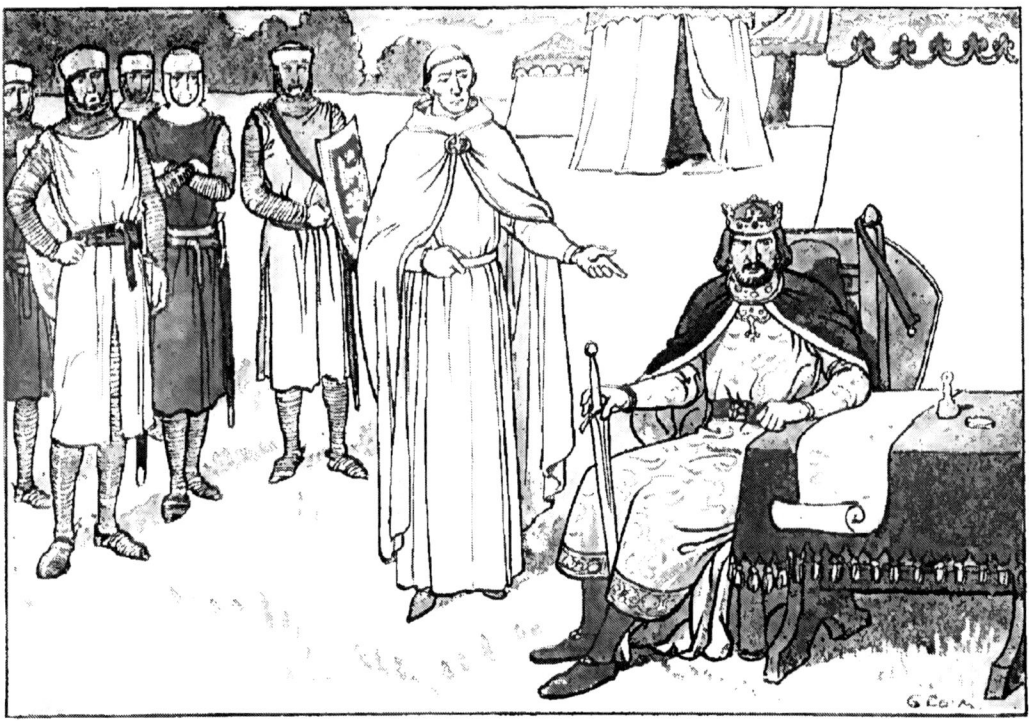

KING JOHN AND THE POPE

When King Richard died, his wicked brother John became king. Nobody liked him. When the Archbishop of Canterbury died, John chose an archbishop himself; but the pope, who lived at Rome, and was head of all the churches, sent another archbishop. His name was Stephen Langton, and he was a very good man; but John would not have him. Then the pope said that all the churches in England should be shut, and there were no services. The people were very sad.

A CARRIAGE IN KING JOHN'S TIME

At last John was so frightened that he gave in to the pope, and he even said he would give England up to the pope and be king under him. So the pope sent a great priest called a cardinal, and John gave up his crown, and then got it back from the cardinal. The English people did not like this, for though the pope was head of the churches, England was not really his to give.

KING JOHN

THE SIGNING OF THE GREAT CHARTER

At last all the people in the country were so angry with John that the chief men said they would fight against him if he did not promise to do better. The new archbishop, Stephen Langton, was very anxious to make the king better to his people. At last they wrote down a great many promises, and they made John say he would keep them, and he had to put a mark under the writing to show that it was a solemn promise. King John never meant to keep his promises, and after he had signed the "Great Charter," as the writing was called, he threw himself upon the ground and kicked and groaned in anger. He died soon afterwards.

71

A KNIGHT WHO GUARDED THE HOLY
SEPULCHRE

AN ENGLISH SHIP IN KING EDWARD I's TIME

THE GREAT EARL SIMON

When King John died, his little son, who was only nine years old, was made king. He was called Henry III. While he was a child wise men looked after the country for him; but when he was a man he had to do it himself. He was not a bad king like his father; but he was not a wise one, and he let the friends whom he liked be cruel to the people. At last a very brave and good man called Earl Simon de Montfort said he would fight against the king, and make him send his foolish friends away. So he did. But after a time the king's son Edward fought for his father against Earl Simon. There was a great battle at a place called Evesham. Earl Simon took the king into the battle beside him. Edward had many more soldiers than Earl Simon, and though the Earl fought bravely, he was at last killed by a soldier who came up behind him and plunged his sword in his back. So Edward won the battle; but he was a wise young man, and told his father to rule the country in the way Earl Simon had wished.

A PREACHER IN EARL SIMON'S TIME

KING EDWARD I AND THE SCOTS

When King Henry III died, Edward became king, and was called Edward I. He was one of the best kings England has ever had. As England had now Ireland, Edward wanted to have Wales and Scotland too. Both these countries are nearer to England than Ireland is, for there is no sea between. When a little girl who was going to be Queen of Scotland died, there were many men who said they should be king. Edward was asked to choose one of them, and he chose one called John Balliol. But Edward wanted John to be king under him, and he said he would, but he did not like to do what the English king told him. So Edward took many soldiers into Scotland, and they fought against the Scotch soldiers and conquered them, and John Balliol was forced to give up his kingdom to Edward. John was taken as a prisoner to London, and the coronation stone on which the Scotch kings used to sit to be crowned was carried to London too, and placed under the coronation chair of the English kings in Westminster Abbey, and there it has been ever since.

A SCOTCH SOLDIER IN KING EDWARD I'S TIME

74

A SOLDIER WATCHING THE ENEMY FROM A CASTLE

THE FIRST PRINCE OF WALES

A CASTLE IN WALES

King Edward had to fight many battles against the Welsh princes before he could get them to take him as king. Even after they had promised they broke their promises, and in the end Edward killed the Prince Llewellyn in battle, and cut his brother David's head off. While he was in Wales, Edward had a little son born to him at a place called Carnarvon, and a story is told that Edward called together the chief Welshmen while his baby was still little, and told them that he would give them the baby as their prince. Later on, the little boy was called Prince of Wales, and the eldest son of every king or queen of England since then has also been called the Prince of Wales.

ROBERT BRUCE, KING OF SCOTLAND

John Balliol had given Scotland up to King Edward, and Englishmen were left to rule the country; but the Scotch people hated them, and they soon rose up to fight against the English. They had several brave Scotchmen to lead them. One of the bravest was a young man named Robert Bruce. He was so anxious to fight the English that he killed his cousin in a church because he would not help him. Many Scotchmen promised to fight under him, and they said he should be their king, and so he was crowned in the big church at a place called Scone, where the Scotch kings were generally crowned. The English kings were always crowned by an archbishop, but sometimes the Scotch kings were crowned by a lady. A lady called the Countess of Buchan crowned Robert Bruce King Edward was very angry; but he was old and sick, and he died while he was on the way to punish the Scotch. So Ireland and Wales belonged to England; but Scotland had a king of its own for many years after.

TWO KNIGHTS FIGHTING

78

THE BRAVE MEN OF CALAIS

King Edward's son and grandson each became king in turn; they were both called Edward too. Edward II was a lazy and cowardly king; but Edward III was a brave soldier. He began a war with the French people which went on long after he was dead, and was called the "Hundred Years' War." He used to take great armies of soldiers over to France, and nearly always the English won the battles. He wanted to take a place called Calais for the English. There was a big strong wall round it, and the people who lived in Calais would

AN OLD ENGLISH GAME CALLED "BLINDMAN'S HOOD"

not open the gates to let King Edward in. So he put soldiers all round the walls, and no one could come out of Calais. When all the food in Calais was eaten, the people could not get anything more to eat. Then they asked King Edward not to kill them if they opened their gates, and gave the place up to him. But King Edward was very angry because they had kept him so long, and he said he would let them off only if they sent six of their chief men to him dressed only in their shirts, with ropes round their necks. They were to give him the keys of the gates, and he would do what he liked to the men. Six brave men offered to go, though they thought King Edward would kill them. When they came before the king, his wife, the good Queen Philippa, was so sorry for them, that she fell on her knees before the king, and begged him to let them go free. Edward could not say "No" to his good and beautiful queen, and so he set the brave men free. But Calais belonged to the English for a long time after that.

THE BLACK PRINCE

King Edward was helped very much by his son, who was called the Black Prince. He was a splendid soldier, and a good man. He once won a great battle against the French, and even took the French king prisoner. But though the prince had conquered King John of France he wanted to show him how much he thought of his bravery, and also because his prisoner was a king, and older than himself, the prince did everything he could to make up to him for his troubles. When the French king was eating, the prince even stood behind him to wait on him at table.

A FRENCH SOLDIER IN THE

F

MEN OF THE TIME OF KING EDWARD II

KING RICHARD II AND THE PEASANTS

When King Edward III died, his grandson, the son of the Black Prince, who was also dead, became King of England. He was called Richard II. He was only a boy, and the people who looked after the country for him did not do it very well. The people had to pay money to them, and they thought it was too much. Many of the poorer people in the country got together in crowds, and said they would fight anyone who tried to make them pay. Many of these peasants, as they were

PEASANTS WORKING IN A FIELD

called, from a part of England called Kent, marched to London to tell the king their troubles. The chief of them was a man called Wat Tyler, but he was not a good man. He burnt many houses in London, and killed some of the great men. King Richard rode out with the Mayor of London to Smithfield, and let Tyler tell him his troubles. While they were talking, Tyler got angry, and the Mayor thought he was going to hurt the king, so he took his dagger and stuck it in Wat Tyler's breast and killed him. The peasants did not know what to do without him. If King Richard had been afraid they might have killed him; but he was a brave boy, and looked straight at them and talked to them while the Mayor rode back into London, and brought some soldiers, and so the king was safe, and the peasants went home.

JOHN WICLIF AND THE BISHOPS

BEGGARS IN THE TIME OF WICLIF

In King Richard II's time there lived a very famous man called John Wiclif. He was a priest; but he began to say things which the other priests thought were not true. He said, too, that the priests should be poor men, and not have beautiful houses and things as many of them had. They said that some of the things he taught about Our Lord were not true. He had to go before a meeting of the Archbishop of Canterbury and other bishops and explain what he meant. We do not know exactly what he said, but he was allowed to go back to his church, and he died soon after. But other men who said the things he said, and would not own they were wrong, were burned to death.

A KING'S JOKE-MAKER OR JESTER

MEN OF WICLIF'S TIME

A LADY AND GENTLEMAN IN THE TIME OF
KING HENRY V

KING HENRY V AND THE FRENCH

Henry IV was not a very happy king. When King Richard was dead some people were sorry, and some tried to take the crown away from Henry; but he kept it. When he died, his son was made king. He was called Henry V. He was a very brave soldier, and he began again the Hundred Years' War with France. He won many battles. The greatest of all was the Battle of Agincourt, when the English had to fight against many more French soldiers than there were English ones. King Henry always said a prayer before a battle, and he thought that God blessed him; but though he won the battles, he could not win France, and it was a pity that so many brave men were killed, and the French people made miserable.

KING HENRY V

JOAN OF ARC

The English had no right to try to take France from the French people. King Henry V died while he was in France, and his son Henry VI was only a baby. The Englishmen who went on with the fighting were not such clever soldiers as King Henry, and a brave country girl, called Joan of Arc, saved France from them. She was just a young peasant girl, and looked after her father's sheep. But she was very good, and she was very sad when she heard how the English soldiers were hurting the French people. While she was saying her prayers she thought that St. Michael and St. Catherine told her to go to the king and save France. So she went, and they gave her clothes like a so'dier's, and a beautiful white banner with a picture of God and two angels on it, and though she was only a girl she led the French soldiers against the English, and won battles for them. Then she took the French king to a place called Rheims, where the French kings were always crowned. When he was crowned, she thought he could finish the war himself, and wanted to go back to her home. But they would not let her. In the end the English took her prisoner, and they gave her up to a French bishop, who thought that she was wicked, and she was burned to death at Rouen. The English too thought she was wicked; but she was a saint.

PEOPLE DRESSED UP TO AMUSE OTHER PEOPLE AT
F   T IMES

94

QUEEN MARGARET AND THE ROBBER

When little King Henry VI grew up he was not a very wise or clever king. He was a good man, but he did not understand how to look after his people. He married a very brave and clever princess, called Margaret of Anjou, and they had one little son called Edward. Some of the people wanted to make another man king, and they fought about it. The wars were called the Wars of the Roses, because those who fought for King Henry wore red roses, and those who fought against him wore white roses. Once during the fighting Queen Margaret had to run away with her little boy. They met a robber. Instead of being frightened, the queen told him who she was, and begged him to show her a place where she and the little prince could hide. The robber was sorry for them, and he thought that the queen was very brave, and so he showed them a safe place to hide. But before the wars were over the poor little prince was killed.

WARWICK THE KINGMAKER, A GREAT FIGHTER IN THE WARS OF THE ROSES

THE FIRST BOOKS PRINTED IN ENGLAND

For hundreds of years after King Alfred's time very few people were taught how to read. The people who could read, like the priests, told them sometimes stories from history, but they had no books, and could not read for themselves.

AN EARLY PRINTING PRESS

Even the people who could read had very few books, and these were not books like we have now, which are printed with machines, but they were books written in by men. These books took a long time to make; but a clever man found out how to print books with machines, and while the Wars of the Roses were still going on a man called William Caxton brought a printing-press to London, and he printed very beautiful books, which rich people could buy and read. Later on, people found out how to print books much more quickly, and then they could sell them for less money. Now even poor people are able to buy nice books for themselves.

G

A MAN WITH A CROSS-BOW AND ONE
OF THE FIRST CANNONS EVER USED

THE PRINCES IN THE TOWER

At the end of the Wars of the Roses, England had a king called Edward IV. He belonged to the red rose side. When he died, his eldest son should have been king; but he was only a boy, and his uncle, who was named Richard, had himself crowned king instead. He took the little prince and his younger brother from their mother and shut them up in the Tower of London; but he was afraid that their friends might fight against him, and so he got a man to kill them, and then he thought he was safe.

KING RICHARD III

THE DEATH OF KING RICHARD III

After King Richard III had killed the little princes people never liked him again. Many people thought that a great man called Henry, Earl of Richmond, should be king, especially the people who had fought for the red rose side in the Wars of the Roses. He got together many soldiers, and fought a battle against Richard at a place called Bosworth Field. Richard was killed, and when he fell his crown fell from his head and rolled on the ground. One of the great men picked it up and put it on the Earl of Richmond's head, and afterwards the people took him for their king, and he was crowned, like all the English kings, in Westminster Abbey. He was called Henry VII.

ANNE, KING RICHARD'S QUEEN

103

AN OLD ENGLISH KITCHEN

LADIES OF THE TIME OF KING HENRY VII

LAMBERT SIMNEL

KING HENRY VII

King Henry VII was rather a wise king. He had some trouble in keeping the crown he had won, but he did keep it. Some people who still liked the white rose side best wanted to make a boy called Edward, Earl of Warwick, king. He was the cousin of the little princes who were killed in the Tower of London. He was kept in prison too; but some of his friends said that he was not, and they showed a pretty boy to the people and said he was the Earl of Warwick. Some of the people fought for him, but Henry's soldiers won, and then they found out that the pretty boy was not the Earl of Warwick; but his name was Lambert Simnel. He was quite a poor boy, and very young, and so King Henry would not punish him. He put him in his kitchen to turn the meat when it was roasting before the fire. So, instead of being a king, Lambert became a kitchen boy, and very likely he was quite happy.

THE FIELD OF THE CLOTH OF GOLD

When Henry VII died his son became king. He was called Henry VIII.

Henry VII had been always very careful over his money, and had saved a great deal. But Henry VIII loved to spend money, and to wear beautiful clothes, and to have the people who lived with him looking merry and beautiful too. Once he went to visit the French king, who was called Francis I, and who was also quite a young man. Both kings wanted to seem richer and more beautiful than the other, and they made their friends and servants dress in beautiful clothes. They met each other in a field, which was ever afterwards known as the Field of the Cloth of Gold, because of the beautiful clothes all the people wore. The kings were very proud and foolish, but the meeting must have been a very beautiful thing to see.

KING HENRY VIII IN ARMOUR

KING HENRY VIII

KING HENRY VIII AND QUEEN KATHARINE
OF ARAGON

THOMAS CROMWELL, WHO HELPED TO
SEND QUEEN KATHARINE AWAY

King Henry VIII was married to a princess from Spain, called Katharine of Aragon. She had been married before, for a short time, to Henry's brother, Arthur, who would have been king if he had not died. Henry could not have married Katharine if the pope had not allowed it, but he did. After many years King Henry began to say that he thought his marriage was not right. He was really tired of poor Queen Katharine. She was good, but she was not very lively, like Henry, and she had only one child, a little girl called Mary. Henry would have liked a boy, to be king after him. At last Henry tried to get the pope to say that the marriage was wrong, and the pope sent a great priest called a cardinal to England. He and Cardinal Wolsey, who was Henry's friend, were to see if what the king thought was true. Queen Katharine had to come before the cardinals and the king. She was very sad, and cried. She threw herself on her knees before the king, and reminded him what a good wife she had been. But Henry did not care. The cardinals did not settle anything; but Henry himself sent Queen Katharine away, and married another wife.

THE GREAT SIR THOMAS MORE

King Henry VIII was very angry with the pope because he would not say the Queen Katharine's marriage was wrong, and he said that the English people should not any longer do what the pope told them. He said too that all the great men must say that his marriage with Queen Katharine was wrong, and his new marriage right. There was one great and good man, called Sir Thomas More, who said he could not say these things, although he would not do any harm to the king. King Henry had once been very fond of Sir Thomas More, and used to go to see him at his house in a part of London called Chelsea. Here Sir Thomas lived with his children and grandchildren. He was the cleverest man in England, and the kindest. He used to say very funny things which made everybody laugh, but they were always kind things. But as he would not say this wrong thing about the king's marriage, Henry said that he should have his head cut off. Sir Thomas's children and grandchildren were terribly sad when he said goodbye to them for the last time. He died very bravely.

THE TOWER OF LONDON

110

THE PILGRIMAGE OF GRACE

When King Henry VIII said that the English people should no longer do what the pope told them, some of them were very sorry, and some of them said that this thing had happened because wicked men were with the king. They said they would fight against these men, and they got ready to march to London. There were priests with them carrying crosses, and pictures of Our Lord and the saints. But King Henry sent a great man called the Duke of Norfolk to tell them that if they went home quietly the king would put everything right. They went to their homes; but afterwards Henry had many of the chief men among them killed, and among them Robert Aske, a gentleman who had been the chief man of all in the Pilgrimage of Grace, as it was afterwards called.

A STREET IN LONDON

LADY JANE GREY

Henry VIII had six wives, one after another. Two he had killed; one died; two he sent away; and one was still alive when Henry himself died. When Henry died, the only son he had became king. He was only a boy. He was called Edward VI. He was clever, but he was not strong, and he soon died too. He had two sisters—Mary, the daughter of Queen Katharine of Aragon, and Elizabeth, the daughter of Henry's second wife, Anne Boleyn, who had had her head cut off. Mary was to be Queen; but some of the chief men did not want her because she was a Catholic, and liked the pope, so they tried to make a beautiful young girl, called Lady Jane Grey, Queen instead; but most of the people wanted Mary, and she was made Queen after all. Lady Jane Grey was put in prison, and soon after, when some people tried again to fight against Queen Mary, she thought it best to have poor Lady Jane killed, and so, though she was quite good, and it was not her fault that they tried to make her queen, she had her head cut off.

THE RIVER THAMES IN QUEEN MARY'S TIME

H

A BEDROOM OF QUEEN MARY'S TIME

QUEEN MARY AND KING PHILIP OF SPAIN

Queen Mary was not a happy Queen. Though she was a Catholic, most of the English people were not. She was very fond of the King of Spain, who was a Catholic too, like all the people of Spain. His name was Philip. The English people did not want Mary to marry him, but she did. They were married in the Cathedral at Winchester, by one of the Catholic bishops. King Philip did not love Mary. He married her because he thought she would make the English people fight on his side in the battles against the French people. Philip would not stay long in England. He went back to Spain, and the Queen was sad, because she loved him. The English people had to help Philip to fight the French; but the French took their town of Calais away from the English, who had had it for many years. This made Queen Mary very sad too. She said that two names were written on her heart—"Philip" and "Calais." She was always thinking of them.

QUEEN MARY

THE BURNING OF ARCHBISHOP CRANMER

A COUNTRYWOMAN OF QUEEN MARY'S TIME

Queen Mary tried to make all the English people Catholics again. Some were very glad; but others thought it was wrong. Some of those who would not become Catholics were burnt to death. There was one Protestant Archbishop, called Thomas Cranmer, who was so frightened to die that he wrote down on a paper that he did not believe any longer in the things the Protestants thought were true. He only wrote this because he hoped the Queen would forgive him, and not have him burnt. But when he knew that he was to be burnt just the same, he spoke out quite bravely, and said he had only written these things because he was afraid to die. But when he was taken to be burnt he held his hand in the fire himself, saying, that it was right that it should be burnt first, because it had written down a lie. Cranmer was dreadfully sorry that he had been so much afraid: but in the end he showed how really brave he was.

119

SIR WALTER RALEIGH, A GREAT MAN OF
ELIZABETH'S TIME

AN IRISH SOLDIER IN THE TIME
OF SHANE O'NEILL

QUEEN ELIZABETH

When Queen Mary died, her half-sister, Elizabeth, became queen. Queen Elizabeth was a great queen, but she was not a very good woman. She was wiser than any of the men who helped her to rule England, and she ruled it well. But when she was not thinking of great things, she was sometimes very silly indeed. She loved to be told that she was beautiful and clever. She was lively like her father Henry VIII, and she loved fine clothes just as he did. She was very proud of her dancing, and sometimes when other queens or kings sent great men with messages to her, she would arrange for them to see her dancing. She would pretend she did not know they were there; but all the time she was wondering what they thought of her dancing.

A GENTLEMAN OF QUEEN ELIZABETH'S COURT

SHANE O'NEILL AND QUEEN ELIZABETH

For hundreds of years after Henry II got Ireland for himself the kings of England could not keep things in order there. In Queen Elizabeth's time the Irishmen in one part of the country were fighting with the Irishmen in other parts. There was one chief man in one part of Ireland who was called Shane O'Neill. He was very strong and brave, and he was not afraid even to come over to England and go to see Elizabeth herself. He could not speak English, but someone explained to the Queen the things he said, and she was very pleased with him. But when he went back to Ireland Shane would not do what Elizabeth wanted him to do. English soldiers were sent to fight him, but he went into another part of Ireland and the Irishmen there killed him.

A CARRIAGE IN THE TIME OF QUEEN ELIZABETH

122

THE MORRICE DANCE. A SPANISH DANCE LEARNED
BY THE ENGLISH PEOPLE

Missing Page

Missing Page

THE GUNPOWDER PLOT

After Queen Elizabeth died, James, the King of Scotland, who was the son of Mary Queen of Scots, became King of England too. He was called James I, and at last the two countries had one king. Queen Elizabeth had punished the Catholics, and now some of them hoped that perhaps King James would become a Catholic like his mother. When they found that James was not going to be any kinder to the Catholics than Queen Elizabeth had been there were just a few Catholics who were

GUY FAWKES AND TWO OTHER GUNPOWDER PLOTTERS

very angry. Some of these made up their minds to kill the king and all the chief men in England. They put bags of gunpowder in a cellar under the Houses of Parliament, where these men used to go to talk about the ruling of the country, and a Spaniard, called Guy Fawkes, stayed in the cellar ready to put a light to the powder at the right time. There would have been an explosion. The Houses of Parliament would have been blown to pieces and all the people inside killed. The Gunpowder Plot, as it was called, was found out in time. Guy Fawkes was dragged out of the cellar, and afterwards he was killed. So were several other Catholics. Ever since those days English children have set off fireworks on the 5th of November because the king and Parliament were saved. Sometimes they make bonfires and burn rag men, which they call "Guys"; but after all, Guy Fawkes was brave in his way and he was not afraid to die.

KING JAMES I READY TO SEND OFF A HAWK TO CATCH OTHER BIRDS

THE SAILING OF THE *MAYFLOWER*

In King James' time some of the Protestants did not like the way the prayers were said in the English churches, and wanted to have churches of their own. In those days people had to say their prayers in the way the king and the chief men of the country told them. At last some of the Protestants, who hated this, made up their minds to leave their homes and sail over the seas to America, which had not long been found out. So they took their wives and children and sailed off in a ship called the *Mayflower* They were very sad at leaving England and going to a strange new land, but they were glad when they got to America and could pray to God in their own way.

KING JAMES I

JENNY GEDDES AND THE ENGLISH PRAYERS

When James I died, his son became king. He was called Charles I. He was a very good man, but he was not a very wise king. He did things that the people hated, and he thought that they had no right to say that anything the king did was wrong. The Scotch people had a different way from the English of saying their prayers in their churches. They thought their way was right. The Archbishop of Canterbury, who was named Archbishop Laud, got the king to say that the Scotch people must have a Prayer Book read in church with prayers in it very like the English prayers. On the first Sunday that the prayers were to be read there were some ladies' maids in the Cathedral at Edinburgh. They used to keep their mistresses' places until they came. One of these women was named Jenny Geddes. When the preacher came out to say the prayers, while she was waiting, Jenny suddenly became very angry

A SOLDIER OF KING JAMES I'S TIME

when she thought of the strange prayers, and she took up her mistress' stool and threw it at the preacher's head. Nearly all the people were sent out of the church, and the prayers were read when there were very few people left. But the Scotch people would not have the English Prayer Book, and in the end they fought against the king.

A LONDON WATCHMAN IN THE TIME OF JAMES I

ARCHBISHOP LAUD

When the Scotch soldiers came to England to fight King Charles, many of the chief men in the Parliament said they would not help the king to fight them. He had to let the Scotch have their own way, and the chief men in Parliament tried to get their own way too. They made the king give up one of his best friends to be killed, and they shut Archbishop Laud up in prison for a long time. The archbishop was, like the king, a good man, but he wanted everybody to do just what he thought good. After a time the men who hated the king cut Archbishop Laud's head off.

A LADY AND GENTLEMAN OF THE TIME OF JAMES I

A LORD MAYOR OF LONDON

THE DEATH OF KING CHARLES I

King Charles and the men who hated him fought many battles. Both sides were very brave, but at last the king's side lost the battles, and the king was taken prisoner. He was shut up in prison, and at last he too had his head cut off. Before he died he was allowed to say good-bye to his two youngest children, a little boy and girl. The little princess was older than her brother, and understood better what was going to happen, and she cried very much. King Charles was very sad but very brave, and when he walked out to have his head cut off in front of his palace at Whitehall, in London, he looked so good and beautiful that all the people were very sad.

THE EARL OF ESSEX, WHO FOUGHT
AGAINST KING CHARLES

KING CHARLES II AND THE OAK-TREE

The eldest son of Charles I was named Charles too. When he became King of England he was called Charles II, but he did not become king until long after his father had died. The men who hated Charles said they would not have a king any more. The chief man among them was Oliver Cromwell, and he fought a battle against Prince Charles. Cromwell won the battle, and the prince had to hide for fear he should have his head cut off too. He went away to France, but before he got away he was often nearly caught. He dressed himself as a poor man. One day he was hiding in a wood when some of Cromwell's soldiers came to look for him. He climbed up into an oak-tree, and the leaves kept the soldiers from seeing him, but he could hear their voices just below him, and he was very glad indeed when they went away. In the end he got away safely to France.

A KITCHEN-MAID IN THE
DAYS OF KING CHARLES I

138

KING CHARLES II

OLIVER CROMWELL AND THE PARLIAMENT

A GENTLEMAN CARRIED IN A SEDAN CHAIR
IN THE TIME OF CHARLES II

For a long time Cromwell tried to rule England with the Parliament. He was a strong man and a little rough, but he knew how to keep order. The men in Parliament talked a great deal, but they did not help to rule the country. Many of the English people wished that they could have a king again, and they did not like Cromwell. At last Cromwell got so tired of the men in Parliament talking and doing nothing, that he went down to the Parliament House and chased the men out. They were afraid of Cromwell and his soldiers, and so they went. The man who kept order in Parliament was called the Speaker, and he used to have a wand called a mace. It was lying on the table in front of him. Cromwell was so angry with the foolish way Parliament had behaved that he called the mace a "bauble" or "toy." "Take away that bauble," he shouted in his angry way, and the mace was taken away to show that the Parliament was ended. After that Cromwell ruled England by himself till he died. He sometimes had a new Parliament, but he always sent it away again. Soon after he died the people were very glad to bring Prince Charles over from France and to have a king again.

THE MERRY KING

King Charles II came back to London on his birthday, the 29th of May. In Cromwell's time people had been dull and sad, but Charles was so lively that he was called the "merry" king. He loved England, and was very happy to be in London again. Charles was very fond of little dogs called spaniels, and he always had two or three with him when he was walking in his gardens or parks. His brother James came back to England too, and the two brothers often used to walk up and down in their great park in London, called St. James's Park. The people used to go into the park too, and were very glad to see their king so happy.

A SELLER IN THE STREETS IN THE DAYS OF
THE MERRY KING

THE GREAT PLAGUE

In Charles II's time a very dreadful thing happened in London. Many people became very ill and died. The illness was called a plague, because it came so suddenly and killed people so quickly. So many died that they could not be buried one at a time, but carts went round, and all the dead people were buried together. Many people suddenly became ill and died in the streets.

After that there was a great fire in London, and many of the beautiful old churches were burnt down. But the fire burnt some of the little dirty streets, and better ones were built. The bad air in the little streets had made the plague much worse.

A JUDGE IN CHARLES II'S TIME

A TRAVELLING TINKER IN THE
DAYS OF BUNYAN

THE WRITER OF "THE PILGRIM'S PROGRESS"

All the people were glad to have Charles II for their king at first, but soon some of them began to be sorry. At first he promised to be good to everyone. There were still some people who wanted to say their prayers in their own way, and they thought the king would let them. But soon the king said that there could not be any churches in which prayers were not said as he wished, and people who went on saying the prayers the king did not like were put in prison. There was a man named John Bunyan, who was a tinker, and mended pots and pans. He had been very lively when he was a boy, and very fond of dancing, but afterwards he was very sorry for those things because he thought they were wrong. He went about telling people to be good, and he tried to get them to say prayers in his way. So he was put in prison. While he was there, although he had never read many books, he himself wrote a wonderful book called "The Pilgrim's Progress."

ONE OF CHARLES II'S
BISHOPS

KING JAMES II

When Charles II died, his brother became king because Charles's wife had not any children. The king was called James II. He was a Catholic, and he tried to make the English people Catholic again. The people did not do anything for some time, but at last a little son was born to James. The people knew that the little baby would be a Catholic, and would be king when his father died. They did not want a Catholic king always, and at last they made up their minds to fight against James, and make another man king. James tried to get away to France on a fishing-boat, but the fishermen guessed that he was the king, and brought him back. In the end James ran away again, and as the people did not know what to do with him now that they had another king they were glad he had gone.

A SOLDIER IN THE REIGN
OF WILLIAM III

THE BRAVE MEN OF LONDONDERRY

KING WILLIAM III

When the English people would no longer have James II for their king, they took a prince called William, who was married to James's daughter Mary. William was king, and Mary was queen. But the Irish people who were Catholics said they would fight for James, and James went from France to Ireland. But there were many Englishmen who had been living in Ireland for a long time but were not really Irish. They were Protestants, and were ready to fight for William and Mary. There was a great deal of fighting. The Catholics put soldiers all round a town called Londonderry, and would not let anybody go in or out. There was the sea on one side of the town, but a great wooden bar was built across so that no English ships could bring food. The people of Londonderry had to eat dogs and cats, and worse things than these, but they would not give their town up. In the end some English ships broke through the bar and brought them food, and then the Catholics went away. There was a great battle fought between William and James. William won, and James went back to France again. The Irish people had to take William for their king.

151

A LADY IN KING WILLIAM'S REIGN

ONE OF THE FIRST FRENCHMEN WHO
WENT TO LIVE IN CANADA

BONNIE PRINCE CHARLIE

A SCOTCH SOLDIER PLAYING
THE BAGPIPES

James II and his family lived for many years in France and Italy. The little baby who had been born to James was called James too, and once when he was grown up he went to Scotland, and some of the Scotch people fought for him, and tried to make him king again, but he did not win the battles, and soon went away again. He was always very sad, and people were not very fond of him. He had a son, also, who was very lively and beautiful, and when he grew up he was called Bonnie Prince Charlie. He went to Scotland many years after his father, and he fought so well, and the Scotch people loved him so much, that he won the battles in Scotland. Then he marched on into England, but the English people were quite happy with their own king, and they fought against Prince Charlie and won the battle. The poor prince had to go away again to Scotland, and even there he had to hide for fear the English soldiers should catch him. He hid among the rocks and in caves on the seashore. A beautiful young lady, called Flora Macdonald, helped him to get back again to France. After that none of James II's family ever tried to become King of England again.

THE TAKING OF QUEBEC

Not long after the English people had begun to go to America and have lands there, some French people went to a part of America near where the English lived. It was called Canada. After many years the English and French in America began to quarrel, and at last English soldiers were sent out to Canada to fight the French. The chief place in Canada was called Quebec. It was built on the top of a hill near a river. One of the chief men who was over the soldiers was called James Wolfe. He was very brave. He wanted to take Quebec from the French. The only way he could do it was to climb up a very little path on the high hill at night, so that the French would not know that he was coming. The path was so little that the soldiers could only go up one behind the other. But in the morning they were all at the top and surprised the French. They fought a great battle, and the English got Quebec, and then all Canada for themselves. But Wolfe was killed in the battle that morning.

A RED INDIAN SELLING FURS TO AMERICANS

154

AN ENGLISH LADY AND GENTLEMAN
IN THE TIME OF WOLFE

THE AMERICANS AND THE ENGLISH TEA

A WATCHMAN

After a long time there came to be many people in America. They had to obey the English king, and do some things which the English Parliament told them. The people in America could not send the things they grew and made to any other country but England. They did not mind this, but some of the men in the English Parliament thought the Americans should do just what they were told about these things, and the Americans thought that they themselves should have *their* own way. The English sent some tea which had come from India. They said the Americans must pay some money, called a tax, when they bought it. The Americans were so angry that they made up their minds to throw all the tea into the sea. Some of them dressed themselves up like Red Indians, the wild people who lived in America before the English went there, and went on the ships and threw all the tea into the water. After that there was a war, but the Americans won, and they said that America should no longer belong to the English. After that they were called the United States of America, but Canada still belonged to the English.

THE DRESSES OF LONG AGO

In the olden times people did not dress as we do now. Before Queen Elizabeth's time clothes were very beautiful, but in her time clothes were made of beautiful silks and other stuff, but the shapes were not so beautiful. Afterwards the dresses became nicer again, but never quite so beautiful as before. In the days when the Americans fought against the English men wore coloured clothes, and they wore wigs of false hair over their own hair, which was cut short. Ladies had their hair puffed out and sprinkled with powder. They also sometimes painted one or two dark spots on their faces, which were called beauty spots. Rich people in those days used to go very often to places where there were springs of water, which they drank to make themselves stronger. They used to have long holidays, and drink the water every day, and spend their time walking in the parks, or playing games of cards in the evenings. They were very lively, but they were often not very good or sensible.

A FRENCH BATTLESHIP

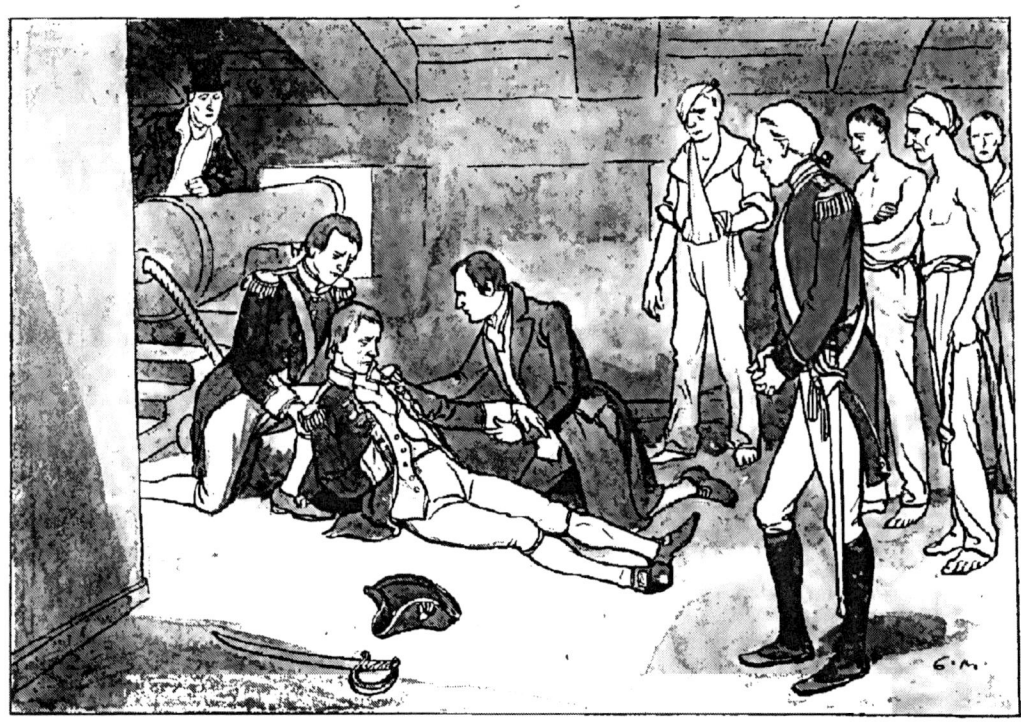

THE GREAT LORD NELSON

About a hundred years ago there was a great French soldier called Napoleon, who wanted to make all the other countries do what the French people told them. He won many great battles, but the English people made up their minds to fight him, and keep England and the other countries free. Napoleon was one of the greatest soldiers who have ever lived. The English had to fight him on the sea and on the land. The greatest soldier the English had on the sea was named Nelson. He was very brave and very lively. He was a little thin man, and was often very ill, but when he was telling his soldiers how to fight he forgot everything else. In one battle one of his eyes was shot out, and after that he had only one eye. In another battle, after this, there was another man who was to tell Nelson what to do. This was not a very brave man, and in the middle of the fight he wanted to stop and let the ships sail away. He made a signal with the flags to tell Nelson this, but Nelson pretended not to see it, and when someone told him about it, he put a telescope, or glass, through which people look to see things better, to his eye, and said he could not see the signal.

AN OFFICER ON A FRENCH BATTLESHIP

He went on fighting, and won the battle. He had put the glass to his blind eye, and so, of course, he could not see the signal. He did this in fun, but all the same he was determined to go on fighting, and to win.

THE DEATH OF NELSON

Later on, Nelson fought the greatest of all his battles. It was against a great many French and Spanish ships, for Spain was one of the countries which France had won. A very great battle was fought. Nelson thought of nothing but how he loved his country. All his men loved him, and he knew that they would take notice of anything he said. So he had a signal made, and all his men on all his ships read the words "England expects every man this day will do his duty" The men made up their minds that they would, and they fought so well that they won a great battle. But Nelson was killed by a shot in his chest. Before he died he asked his friend, Captain Hardy, to kiss him. The last words he said were "Thank God, I have done my duty."

AN ENGLISH SAILOR IN THE TIME OF NELSON

L

AN OFFICER ON AN ENGLISH
BATTLESHIP

CHARLES JAMES FOX AND THE SLAVES

In the days when English people first went to America, some parts of that country were too hot for them to work very hard. So black men, from a country called Africa, were stolen away from their homes and taken over to America. The white men bought them, and made them do the hardest work. The black men were slaves. They had to do just what their masters told them, and cruel masters often used to beat them. The slaves could not leave their masters, but were bought and sold just as though they were animals, and not men. Some of the masters were kind to their slaves, but after a time people began to see that it was not right that one man should belong to another. At last the English Parliament said that black men must not be sent any more to America, and later on, the slaves who were already in America were set free. One of the people who tried hardest to have the slaves set free was Charles James Fox. He was a great man, and very kind. He often used to speak in Parliament, saying how cruel it was to make people slaves.

A PEASANT IN THE TIME OF C. J. FOX

THE BURIAL OF SIR JOHN MOORE

One of the chief men who fought against the French on land was Sir John Moore. He did not fight against Napoleon himself, but he fought in Spain against the soldiers whom Napoleon had sent there. He was expecting some more soldiers in ships from England, and had a long way to go to meet them. He had to fight all the time he was marching to the sea. When he got there the ships had not come. There was a great battle, and the English won. They went on the ships, and sailed back to England, but Sir John Moore was killed in the battle, and was buried in the night. A poet wrote a beautiful piece of poetry about him which most children learn when they go to school.

AN ENGLISH OFFICER
WHO FOUGHT UNDER
SIR JOHN MOORE

ONE OF THE FIRST POSTMEN

TWO LADIES AT THE TIME OF THE
BATTLE OF WATERLOO

THE BATTLE OF WATERLOO

THE DUKE OF WELLINGTON

Napoleon was perhaps the greatest soldier who has ever lived. If he had been fighting only for what was right he would most likely never have lost a battle. But when he tried to have all the other countries for himself, they got very angry, especially the English. The greatest soldier who fought Napoleon on land was the Duke of Wellington. Napoleon fought many battles, but at 'last he had to give in. The last battle he fought was the Battle of Waterloo. Wellington, with the Germans to help him, won the battle, and Napoleon had to ride quickly away. He stayed a short time at a cottage to warm himself, and one of his soldiers saw that he was crying, because he had fought his last great battle and lost it. Soon afterwards he gave himself up as a prisoner. He was sent to live in a place with water all round, and watched all the time, so that he could not get away. He had tried to make himself master of all the countries, and he died a prisoner.

THE FIRST POLICEMEN

Nearly a hundred years ago places looked very different from what they do now. The streets were not so safe, even for big men and women, much less little children. Now there are always plenty of policemen to look after people in the streets. But in those days the streets were often full of bad men and thieves. In some places, especially in some parts of London, thieves stood in little crowds, and took things from people who passed. Often they took watches and money. At last a great man in Parliament, called Sir Robert Peel, said that strong, big men should be chosen to keep the streets safe. They were called "Policemen," but some people in fun called them "Peelers" and "Bobbies," and sometimes you hear boys still calling policemen by those names.

A GENTLEMAN IN THE DAYS
OF SIR ROBERT PEEL

TWO OF THE FIRST FIREMEN

CHILDREN WHO WENT TO WORK

Long ago nearly everything that people use —stuff to make clothes, and things like that— used to be made by people at home or in small workrooms. Then, about a hundred years ago, machines were made, which could make things much more quickly than people could with their hands. These machines were put in big workrooms. Some people had to look after them, and these used to go and work all day in the big workrooms. It was found out that quite little children could do some of the work, putting things in and out of the machines. So poor little children used to be sent to do the work. They used to go in the morning, sometimes before the sun was up, and stay all day in the big ugly workrooms until night. They must have been very tired and sad, and many of them got ill and died. At last people began to think that it was a terrible thing for children to live like this, and now the king and Parliament will not allow children to be sent to work. Everyone knows it is much better for them to go to school and have time to play, and so grow up strong and wise men and women.

A BEADLE. A MAN WHO USED TO LOOK AFTER CHILDREN IN POORHOUSES

QUEEN VICTORIA

Our king to-day is called George V. The king before him was his father, King Edward VII. Before King Edward we had a queen, the great Queen Victoria. She was queen for a great many years, from the time she was quite a young girl, until she was a very old woman. When her uncle King William IV died, in the middle of the night, two of the greatest gentlemen in the land came to tell Victoria that she was now queen. She was in bed, but got up to receive them with a shawl thrown over her nightdress. She looked so young, with her hair hanging down her back, that the gentlemen felt they loved their new queen very much. Everybody else loved the girl-queen too, and she soon showed what a good and sensible queen she was going to be.

CHILDREN WHEN VICTORIA WAS FIRST QUEEN

179

M

PRINCE ALBERT, THE HUSBAND OF
QUEEN VICTORIA

FLORENCE NIGHTINGALE

Many years ago there was a war between some people called Russians and others called Turks. The Russians wanted to take some of the Turks' land from them. This was not right. So the English and French people sent soldiers to help the Turks. The soldiers were very brave, but their leaders did not know much about the far-off country where they had to fight. When the winter came, there was not enough food for the soldiers, and they had not enough clothes. Many of them were terribly ill, and there was no one to look after them. Then a very good and kind lady, called Florence Nightingale, went out to the soldiers with some nurses, and they did all they could to make the sick soldiers comfortable and better. The poor soldiers loved Miss Nightingale very much, and the English people have always been proud of her.

A SOLDIER OF THE TIME OF
FLORENCE NIGHTINGALE

THE SCOTCH SOLDIERS AT LUCKNOW

There is a very hot country over the seas called India. It belongs to England, but the people who live there are not English. They are men with brown skins.

LADY AND GENTLEMAN IN THE
MIDDLE OF THE REIGN OF
QUEEN VICTORIA

They are not wild people, but they do everything in a different way from English people. There are some English people who live there to see that the brown people do what the English king and Parliament tell them. Once some of the people in India thought that the English had been unkind to them, and they made up their minds to fight the English. There were not many English, and before any more could be sent from England many of the English people in India, even the women and children, were killed. There was one place, called Lucknow, where there were many women and children. The Hindoos were all round the place, and the English had very little left to eat. They thought they would have to give in to the Hindoos, but there was a Scotch girl who was maid to an English lady. She was lying ill, and the lady was looking after her, when suddenly the girl called out that she heard the music of Scotch soldiers coming. People thought she was dreaming, because no one else could hear it. But she was right. The Scotch soldiers were on their way, and came in time to save them.

183

QUEEN VICTORIA

A YEOMAN OF THE GUARD, ONE OF
THE SOLDIERS WHO HAVE TO
LOOK AFTER THE KING

THE BURIAL OF KING EDWARD VII

KING EDWARD VII

King Edward VII was a great king, and a kind man, and when he died people all over the world were very sorry. When he was dead his body was put for a few days in Westminster Abbey, and the people were allowed to go to do him honour. But he was buried at a place called Windsor, and when the king was taken through the streets of London to be put in the train to go to Windsor, there was a great procession. The streets were crowded with people to see it. The king's horse, and his dog, Cæsar, were in the procession, and other kings had come from their own countries to show how much they thought of King Edward. The new King George was there, of course, and Queen Alexandra, the dead king's wife, riding in her carriage. Everyone was very sad, but it was a great comfort to think how much people had loved the king.

THE CROWNING OF KING GEORGE AND QUEEN MARY

After a time the new king, George V, and his wife, Queen Mary, were crowned in Westminster Abbey. People felt happy again, because they knew they had a good and clever king, and a kind queen. The king and queen wore beautiful dresses or robes, and so did all the great nobles and their wives.

QUEEN ALEXANDRA

A HINDOO PRINCE

THE MEN WHO GO THROUGH THE AIR

QUEEN MARY

Now people can not only go quickly over the sea in ships, and over the land in trains, but quite lately some very clever men have found out how to go quickly through the air. They sail right up into the air in things called aeroplanes. The airmen are very brave, because there are often accidents. They do not know yet how to manage aeroplanes as well as they do ships and trains. Once, not so long ago, some people got an airman to carry letters with him from a place in London to a place called Windsor. Perhaps some day the aeroplanes will be used for this and other useful things.

KING GEORGE AND THE INDIAN PRINCES

One of the biggest countries which belongs to England is India. It is very hot, and poor English people do not go out there, but just a few English people who help to rule the country. There are a great many Indian princes. A short time ago, King George and Queen Mary went out to India, and the Indian princes went and bowed down before them to do them honour. Some of them brought presents, and it was a very fine sight. The king and queen wish India to be happy, and all the other lands they rule too.

KING GEORGE

PRINCE EDWARD

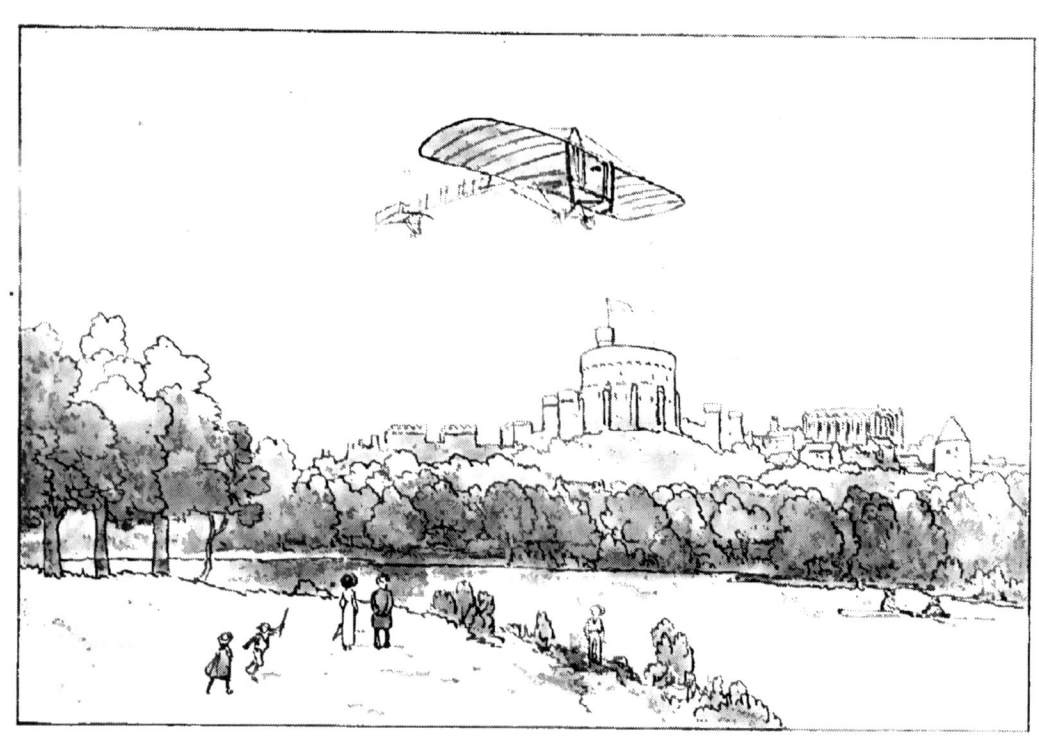

Lightning Source UK Ltd.
Milton Keynes UK
172446UK00006B/37/P